Mix it Up!

The Science of Chemistry

Sunnie Kim and Lisa Melton

Illustrated by Dirk Wunderlich and Phil Ortiz

Science Kids

LPC
GROUP

ISBN: 1-891418-15-9

Contributing Writers: Sunnie Kim, Lisa Melton, & Dennis Lamour
Contributing Artists: Dirk Wunderlich & Phil Ortiz

Learning Activity Book™

Manufactured in the United States of America

Note to Parents and Teachers ◄···········

Science is an integral part of our everyday lives. More so now than ever before in our history, it is critical that children grasp scientific concepts so they may succeed in the challenges of the future. The **SCIENCE-KIDS LEARNING ACTIVITY BOOK** series builds scientific literacy through a systematic presentation of the National Academy of Sciences' **National Science Education Content Standards**.

The second title in the series, *Mix It Up!,* presents a wonderful opportunity for young readers to learn about the world of chemistry. The lively and humorous text is sure to entice youngsters into this world, and once there, they'll be fascinated! Some of the scientific concepts covered are:

> **For Teachers:** Read each section together as a class. Encourage questions about concepts or words that aren't clear to your students. Once the class reading is completed, students can work independently on the activities in that section.

⇨ the beginning of chemical experimentation
⇨ atoms and the elements
⇨ chemical properties
⇨ chemical bonds
⇨ molecules and compounds
⇨ molecular structures
⇨ chemical reactions

How to Use This Book

Mix It Up! is divided into different sections, as indicated by each new headline. Tell your child or students to pay attention to the words printed in bold. These are new science terms for that section. By the end of each section, readers can "Check Out the Science Words!"—a list of the new vocabulary words they've encountered.

In checking off each word, children can monitor their progress on mastering concepts.

Group Projects: Some of the activities in *Mix It Up!* may be expanded for group projects in the classroom. These are identified with a C . Please review in advance the group activities to be sure all the materials needed are on hand for your students to use. You can split up the students into groups. Encourage the kids to talk about the activity, question each other, and especially to draw pictures of what they've learned. Modeling the scientific ideas on paper will go a long way toward understanding each lesson.

Throughout the book, children will also find interesting, skill-building activities that aid in learning science—and especially in having fun. The activities, and experiments, too, are designed to reinforce the scientific concepts your child or students are learning; they'll also encourage children to explore chemistry in everyday life. The answers to the exercises can be found near the end of this book.

Last, but definitely not least, a certificate of completion awaits your child or student on the last page of *Mix It Up!* When the book has been completed, reward your young reader with this honor. Children develop a sense of academic achievement when their efforts at learning are valued and appreciated. The recognition will also give your child or student a feeling of success and thereby promote self-esteem.

As parents and teachers, we know children have the amazing gift of curiosity. We can make good use of that curiosity by keeping reading time enjoyable. Therefore, when you work with your child or students on this book, captivate their interest by making the experience creative and positive. Don't worry about being able to answer all the questions your child and students come up with. Not even a scientist could do that! Simply read with them, listen to their comments and questions, and discuss the illustrations and examples provided. Especially do some experiments together. Have fun!

Hₒw Did it All Start?

IMAGINE A TIME LONG AGO, about 10,000 years in the past, well before people lived in cities or children went to school. People saw all sorts of things around them. They looked at rocks, metals, and plants and wondered what useful things could be made with them. Could they be used just as they were? Or could they be changed in some way and made even more useful?

Questions like these led people to **experiment** on the **substances** around them. And that was how **chemistry** was born.

Presto Change-o

In everyday life, changes happen all around us all the time. Leaves change color, snow melts, raw food gets cooked into something you'd want to eat! Think about how changes happen, then answer these questions.

❶ How could you change the shape of an ice cube? _get a Different_ _shaped ice cube thing,_

❷ What could you add to milk to change its color? _____
_____

❸ Have you ever made anything with leaves, twigs, petals, or any other part of a plant? What was it? Did you change the plant part in any way? _____
_____

❹ Have you ever baked a cake or cookies? What happened to the dough as it heated up? _____

❺ What happens when you put a spoonful of sugar into some tea? _____
_____

Chemistry, like astronomy, geology, biology, and physics, is a science. Chemistry is about:

⇨ Observing the different substances there are in the world.

⇨ Why and how substances are different from each other, and

⇨ Ways they can change to form new substances.

What's the Difference?

As you read through these pages, you'll run into the words **chemical, material,** *and* **substance** *again and again. What do they all mean? Well, in chemistry, that's easy. They all mean same thing!*

Do You Know 'Em?

Do you know what the different sciences are about? What does each study? Read through all the definitions below. Write the letter of the correct science in the blank where it belongs.

❶ ___ This is the study of stars, planets, moons, and other objects in outer space.

❷ ___ In this science, people study living things, such as plants and animals.

❸ ___ This science is about the earth and what it's made of: rocks, mountains, valleys, and so forth.

❹ ___ Scientists in this area examine the fossil remains of animals that lived long ago.

❺ ___ In this science, people study why substances are different from each other and how they react to form new substances.

a. geology

b. chemistry

c. astronomy

d. biology

e. paleontology

CHECK OUT THE SCIENCE WORDS!

Do you remember reading about each of the words below? When you think you know the meaning of a word, put a ✓ in the box next to it.

- ❑ **experiment**
- ❑ **substance**
- ❑ **chemistry**
- ❑ **science**
- ❑ **material**
- ❑ **chemical**
- ❑ **tanning**

By about 8,000 years ago, people had gotten very good with chemistry. Using a variety of materials, they became skilled at different crafts. They could melt metals from solid to liquid, and in that way change the shape of the solid. They could mix two or more metals together to make a new metal.

In a practice called **tanning**, people could make leather out of animal skins. They also knew how to make colorful dyes out of plants, and to brew beverages from them, too.

All of these crafts had one thing in common: People took one kind of material and made it into another. That's chemistry!

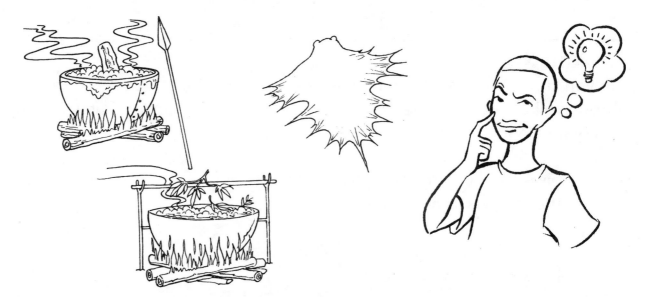

Time Line

350 million years ago (MYA)	270 MYA	150 MYA	100 MYA	30,000 to 20,000 years ago	10,000 to 8,000 years ago
Bacteria first appear on Earth	The first fish appear in the ocean	Dinosaurs roam the planet	Birds, mammals, and humans first appear	People hunt and gather their food; paintings drawn in caves	People begin to grow crops; animals are domesticated; the chemical crafts begin.

The Alchemists

IF YOU DISCOVERED YOU HAD the power to chemically change one material into another, what would you try to make? If you're like some people who lived long ago, you'd try to make the beautiful substance we call gold. That's called alchemy, making gold out of less valuable metals.

Can *You* Make Gold?

The word, that is! In just five moves, you can turn the word LEAD into the word GOLD. Here's how: For each step, change only one letter at a time. Each change must make a real new word. The first step is done for you.

	LEAD	
step 1:	LEND	(A changed to N)
step 2:		
step 3:		
step 4:		
step 5:		
step 6:		
step 7:		
step 8:	GOLD	

Do you remember reading about each of the words below? When you think you know the meaning of a word, put a ✓ in the box next to it.

❑ **alchemy**

❑ **alchemist**

❑ **element**

Today we know what the alchemists did not: It's impossible to change one **element** into another element. And that's what gold is, an element. Are you wondering what an element is? Read on . . .

To make gold, alchemists tried using other metals, such as lead, copper, and zinc. They heated these other substances, poured acid over them, mixed them with a bunch of different chemicals—all to try to get that lustrous result: gold.

I Knew That

Learning all about science is easy. Decoding ancient secret messages can be tricky! Use the shape code below to help you discover a very old secret message.

A	B	C	D	E	F	G	H	I	J	K	L	M
◗	★	Ⓒ	✈	❀	✗	☛	♥	✏	▼	✉	☆	✳

N	O	P	Q	R	S	T	U	V	W	X	Y	Z
☞	▲	◆	❖	✧	✪	✸	✿	✔	✖	✂	♡	◆

The year is 8,000 B.C. Today's chemistry lesson is . . .

WATER DO NOT BURN.

TREE BURN TOO FAST!

The Chemical Basics

AN ELEMENT IS A **PURE** substance, which means it isn't mixed with anything else. Gold, silver, aluminum, zinc, hydrogen, oxygen, and about a hundred other different substances are kinds of elements. Each element is *unique*. That means it is one-of-a-kind, unlike any other element.

WHERE DO YOU PUT YOUR DIRTY DISHES?

IN THE **ZINC**, OF COURSE!

Material Mix Up

The alchemists did a lot of mixing of substances to try and make something new. Now it's your turn to do some mixing of words, that is! In each sentence below, a word or two or three is out of place. It's your job to move it to just the right place for the sentence to make sense. Rewrite the correct sentence on the line provided.

1. science chemistry is a.

   _____

2. why and how substances are different each other from chemistry is about.

   _____

3. It is possible to change one not element into another element.

   _____

4. gold was one of the substances that alchemists tried to turn into lead.

   _____

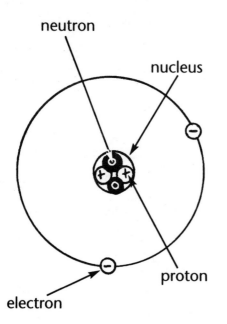

So, how are the elements different from each other? For that answer, let's look at the tiniest bit of an element you can have: an **atom**. Now we're really getting down to the basics of chemistry. Atoms are made of **protons (+)**, **neutrons (o)**, and **electrons (-)**. The protons and neutrons are jammed into the center of the atom, inside the **nucleus**. The electrons float around the atom *outside* the nucleus.

Elements are one-of-a-kind in the number of protons they have in their nucleus. For example, an atom of the element hydrogen has just 1 proton.

Did You Know?

Steel, brass, air, and water are not elements! These materials are each made up of many elements. Steel is made mostly of iron, plus a little bit of carbon, manganese, chromium, nickel, copper, and other elements. Brass is made of the elements copper and zinc, with small amounts of other elements mixed in. Air is mostly nitrogen and oxygen, with lesser amounts of argon, helium, and other elements floating around. Water is one of the simplest substances. It's made up of just two elements, hydrogen and oxygen.

An atom of the element oxygen has 8 protons in it. An atom that has 79 protons is gold. A pure gold nugget is made up of many gold atoms, and each and every one of those atoms has 79 protons in it. What's more, each and every one of those atoms behaves the same way—like gold.

That brings us to one of the main ideas in chemistry. All atoms with the same number of protons are the same element, and they all behave the same way chemically. In other words, they have the same **properties**.

CHECK OUT THE SCIENCE WORDS!

Do you remember reading about each of the words below? When you think you know the meaning of a word, put a ✓ in the box next to it.

- ❑ **pure**
- ❑ **atom**
- ❑ **proton**
- ❑ **neutron**
- ❑ **electron**
- ❑ **nucleus**
- ❑ **properties**

Break the Code!

You've heard of gold, silver, and copper, and possibly even mercury, zinc, and potassium. Did you know these elements are all metals? Many, many other elements are also metals. Some of them have unusual names! Use the shape code below to help you discover the names of several other metallic elements.

A	B	C	D	E	F	G	H	I	J	K	L	M
◗	★	©	✈	❀	✗	☞	♥	✐	▼	✉	☆	✳

N	O	P	Q	R	S	T	U	V	W	X	Y	Z
☞	▲	◆	❖	✧	★	✻	❀	✔	✖	✂	♡	◆

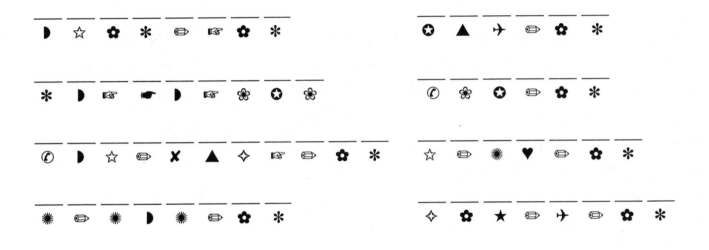

A Metal Is a Metal Is a Metal (or Is It?)

When you think of metal, do you think of something strong, hard, and solid? Do you think of something silvery? Well, metals are no different than any other substance: They can have very different qualities, or properties. Did you know, for example, that three metals—mercury, cesium, and gallium—are liquid at room temperature? And while it's true that most metals are silvery looking, copper is a reddish-brown and gold is yellow. Most metals also bend well, but a few, such as chromium and bismuth, are brittle, which means they'd rather just break than bend.

It's Elementary, My Dear ◄ ·············

Whether you realize it or not, you already know a lot about properties. Why? Because you use your senses!

Your eyes tell you a whole lot about properties. You can *see* that different substances have different colors, sizes, and shapes.

You can *feel* differences, too. Some elements are hard, such as iron or titanium, while others are soft and chalky, such as calcium.

Sometimes, you can even *smell* the difference between elements!

CHECK OUT THE SCIENCE WORDS!

Do you remember reading about each of the words below? When you think you know the meaning of a word, put a ✓ in the box next to it.

- ❑ **proton**
- ❑ **electron**
- ❑ **neutron**
- ❑ **charge**
- ❑ **positive**
- ❑ **negative**
- ❑ **neutral**
- ❑ **nucleus**
- ❑ **weight**

DID SOMEONE ASK ABOUT PROPERTIES?

NO. NOT THAT KIND OF PROPERTIES. WE'RE TALKING ABOUT PHYSICAL AND CHEMICAL PROPERTIES OF SUBSTANCES.

Chlorine has a strong smell. It's used to clean our drinking water. And sulfur, combined with two hydrogens (hydrogen sulfide) has the most pleasant odor of all—rotten eggs!

Atomic Crossword

This crossword puzzle is packed with words you've learned about atoms and chemicals. The ACROSS clues are below and the DOWN clues are on the next page. Read each clue and fill in the puzzle on page 17. If you need help, turn to the Word Box below.

ACROSS

3. It's here where you'll find protons and neutrons.

5. The smallest bit of an element you can have is an _____.

6. The tiny particle that floats outside the nucleus in an atom.

8. Another word for chemical.

9. This word also means material.

Word Box

atom
chemistry
electron
element
material
neutron
nucleus
proton
substance

Can you think of any other properties scientists might use to tell the elements apart? Well, each element has its own **weight**. Each has a certain **melting temperature**, the temperature at which it changes from a solid to a liquid. Each element also has a **boiling temperature**, the temperature at which it boils from a liquid to a gas.

DOWN

1. One of the particles inside an atom's nucleus is called this.

2. The other particle inside an atom's nucleus is called this.

4. An _____ is the simplest substance you can have.

7. This is the science of chemical change.

Another important property is **density**. That's how much "stuff"—no matter what the stuff is—is crammed into a certain amount of space, or **volume**. If you had a box full or dirt, a solid, it would be a lot heavier than a box full of air, a gas. That's because more atoms are packed into dirt than air. We can say that the density of a box of dirt is greater than the density of a box of air.

We *measure* properties in different ways. We've already talked about one way—your senses. Your eyes, for example, are your very own measuring tools for comparing color or shininess or size. We also use scales, rulers, thermometers, and lots of other tools besides our senses.

⇨ ⇨ ⇨ *Go to page 21!*

That's Heavy!

As you've learned, different elements have different properties, such as hardness, density, or reactivity (the ability to react with other substances to form new ones). Below are four substances, all the same size and shape (a cube).

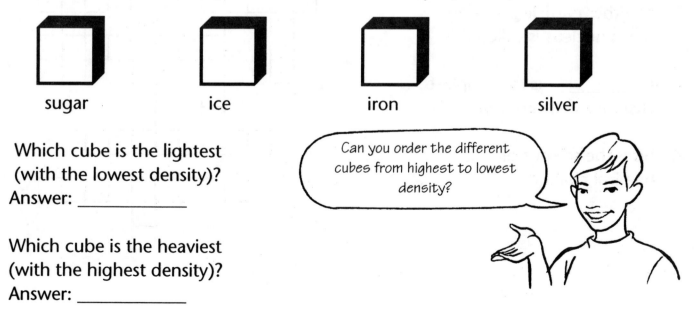

sugar   ice   iron   silver

Which cube is the lightest (with the lowest density)?
Answer: _____

Can you order the different cubes from highest to lowest density?

Which cube is the heaviest (with the highest density)?
Answer: _____

EXPERIMENT: A Cup Full of Pockets C

In this experiment, you'll discover that 1 + 1 does not always equal 2. How can that be? You'll see!

What you'll need:
- water
- rubbing alcohol
- measuring cup
- two identical drinking glasses
- spoon

What to do:

1. Measure out exactly 1 cup of water in the measuring cup. Pour it into one of the drinking glasses.

2. Next measure out a second cup of water, and pour it into the first glass. You should have exactly two cups of water in your glass.

3. Now let's do a little mixing. First measure out exactly 1 cup of water and pour it into the second glass. To that, add exactly 1 cup of the rubbing alcohol. Stir the alcohol and water together with the spoon.

4. Place the two glasses side by side and compare the amount of liquid in them. Do they have the same volume? Or does one have more liquid than another? How could that be, since you poured exactly two cups into both glasses?

Why?

In the second glass, even though you added 1 cup of alcohol to 1 cup of water, you didn't end up with 2 cups of liquid. How very strange! Believe it or not, water contains pockets of empty space. Well, water and rubbing alcohol have different structures. Water can't fill its own pockets, so when you add one cup of water to another, you get . . . two cups of water. Alcohol, however, can fill the empty pockets. When you add a cup of alcohol to water, you get . . . less than two cups. So, which is more dense or packed? The water or the alcohol-plus-water?

EXPERIMENT: Eggs, Please! C

Which do you think is more dense, plain water or saltwater? What sort of experiment could you do to find out? In the following experiment, a couple of eggs come in handy for answering that question!

What you'll need:
- 2 clear plastic cups
- table salt
- 2 eggs
- water
- measuring spoon

What to do:

1. Fill the plastic cups about half full with water. To one of the cups, add 3 tablespoons of salt and stir until the salt dissolves.

2. Carefully drop an egg into the cup with only water in it. What happens to the egg?

3. Next drop an egg into the cup with saltwater. What happens to the egg this time?

Another important property is **density**. That's how much "stuff"—no matter what the stuff is—is crammed into a certain amount of space, or **volume**. If you had a box full or dirt, a solid, it would be a lot heavier than a box full of air, a gas. That's because more atoms are packed into dirt than air. We can say that the density of a box of dirt is greater than the density of a box of air.

We *measure* properties in different ways. We've already talked about one way—your senses. Your eyes, for example, are your very own measuring tools for comparing color or shininess or size. We also use scales, rulers,

CHECK OUT THE SCIENCE WORDS!

Do you remember reading about each of the words below? When you think you know the meaning of a word, put a ✓ in the box next to it.

- ❑ melting temperature
- ❑ boiling temperature
- ❑ density
- ❑ volume
- ❑ reactivity

Yep, That's a Property

Hidden in the puzzle are all the words from the word list below. Find and circle them. The words can be up and down, across, or diagonal.

SHININESS	WEIGHT
HARDNESS	DENSITY
SIZE	SHAPE
COLOR	SMELL
BOILING TEMP.	
MELTING TEMP.	

A	C	T	I	O	R	K	W	Z	P	A	S	O
L	U	X	S	H	A	P	E	O	R	B	O	S
T	G	D	T	M	Z	E	I	R	O	S	M	I
U	M	E	L	T	I	N	G	T	E	M	P	U
R	K	N	S	H	U	O	H	O	T	E	T	H
L	W	S	U	M	C	V	T	R	I	L	K	A
T	E	I	S	I	D	I	H	C	O	L	O	R
E	E	T	H	M	V	M	O	T	E	I	A	D
A	M	Y	O	C	T	E	T	E	R	Y	Z	N
D	O	U	R	B	R	E	T	S	O	M	M	E
I	R	R	T	S	H	I	N	I	N	E	S	S
S	C	O	M	R	C	O	R	Z	E	I	K	S
B	O	I	L	I	N	G	T	E	M	P	E	R

Take a Guess

Though you're only just beginning to learn about the properties of substances, you can take your best guess: Which objects are softest? Which hardest? Which are lightest? And so on. In each row, put the items in order, putting your numbers in the circles provided. Good luck!

Number the items from softest ⇨ hardest.

○ sandpaper   ① fur   ○ soil   ○ leaf

Number the items from lightest ⇨ heaviest.

① flour   ○ sugar   ○ cooking oil   ○ honey

Number the items from dullest ⇨ shiniest.

○ marble   ① wood   ○ concrete   ○ glass

Number the items from least transparent ⇨ most transparent.

○ paper   ① aluminum foil   ○ glass   ○ plastic

The Elements Team Up ◄••••••••••••••••••••••

PEOPLE USE WORDS TO SPEAK to each other. Atoms "speak" to each other, too— through their electrons. When two atoms come close together, the electrons decide if the two atoms would be a good match. If yes, then the atoms team up and form a **chemical bond**, which is kind of a connection. A chemical bond is made of two electrons. Atoms can form chemical bonds a couple of different ways:

❶ One atom can come along and take an electron right off of another atom. When that happens, the two atoms form an **ionic bond**.

❷ Two atoms can say, "Let's share our electrons!" If they do, the atoms form a **covalent bond**.

Of course, atoms don't *really* talk to each other, but in a way, their electrons are always communicating. When two or more atoms decide to team up and form bonds, they become a **molecule**. You can think of the bond-forming process this way: Different atoms have different "electron-attracting powers." Some have powers so great that they can steal an electron from another atom and in that way form a bond. Chlorine is like that. Whenever it gets near another atom, such as sodium, it steals an electron. Sodium, on the

Kaboom!

Using words from the Word Box, fill in the blanks to find out something very interesting about sodium.

Remember this _____ . When you grow up and are working in a
$\quad\quad\quad$ 11

_____ , don't place _____ , not even a little tiny piece of it, in _____ .
$\quad$ 8 $\quad\quad\quad\quad\quad\quad$ 2 $\quad\quad\quad\quad\quad\quad\quad\quad\quad\quad\quad$ 1

If you do, you might have an _____ . That's because this metal has just a
$\quad\quad\quad\quad\quad\quad\quad\quad\quad\quad$ 9

single outer _____ , which the _____ in a _____
$\quad\quad\quad\quad\quad$ 7 $\quad\quad\quad\quad\quad\quad$ 4 $\quad\quad\quad\quad$ 1

molecule loves to _____ . In fact, the _____ steals the
$\quad\quad\quad\quad\quad\quad\quad$ 6 $\quad\quad\quad\quad\quad\quad\quad$ 4

_____ quite violently. The _____ and _____
7 $\quad\quad\quad\quad\quad\quad\quad\quad\quad\quad\quad$ 2 $\quad\quad\quad\quad$ 1

molecules react to form _____ hydroxide and _____
$\quad\quad\quad\quad\quad\quad\quad\quad$ 2 $\quad\quad\quad\quad\quad\quad\quad\quad\quad$ 3

gas. The _____ also creates a lot of heat, so much so
$\quad\quad\quad$ 10

that the _____ gas may catch _____ —kaboom!
$\quad\quad\quad$ 3 $\quad\quad\quad\quad\quad\quad\quad\quad$ 5

Word Box
1 water
2 sodium
3 hydrogen
4 oxygen
5 fire
6 steal/steals
7 electron
8 laboratory
9 explosion
10 reaction
11 warning

other hand, has very little electron-attracting power. It easily gives up an electron to a nearby chlorine atom. So, after a chlorine atom meets up with a sodium atom, the result is a transfer of an electron, from sodium to chlorine.

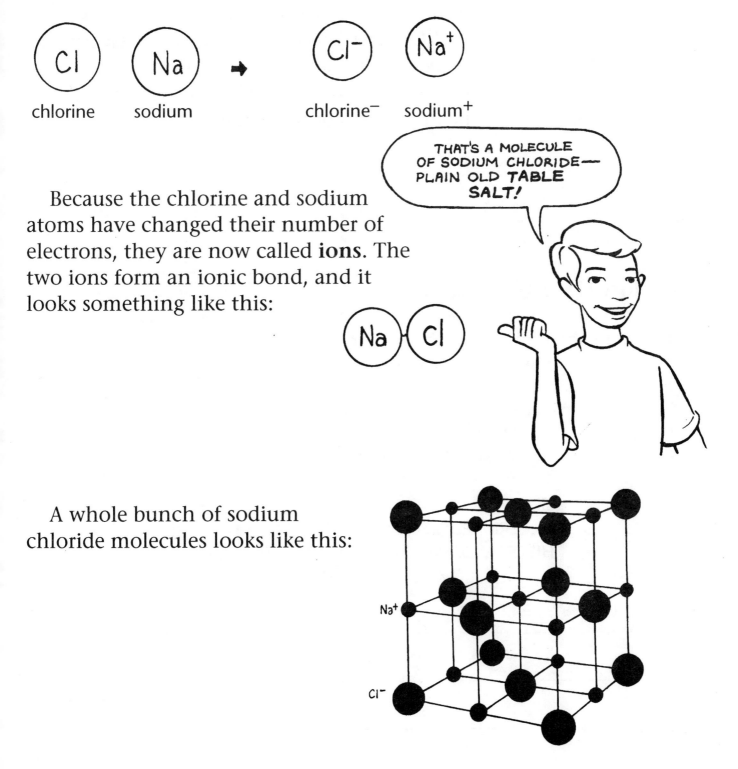

chlorine   sodium   chlorine⁻   sodium⁺

THAT'S A MOLECULE OF SODIUM CHLORIDE— PLAIN OLD **TABLE SALT!**

Because the chlorine and sodium atoms have changed their number of electrons, they are now called **ions**. The two ions form an ionic bond, and it looks something like this:

A whole bunch of sodium chloride molecules looks like this:

Na⁺

Cl⁻

What happens when atoms with the same electron-attracting power come near each other? What if neither atom is strong enough to steal an electron from the other? What happens is that the two atoms "decide" to share their electrons. This equal sharing results in a covalent bond.

When two atoms can share their electrons by bonding, they become more stable. That means they are less likely to react with other nearby atoms or molecules.

They Just Have to Steal!

Here's something more to learn about atoms and their powers. Circle every other letter (or symbol) in the puzzle below. Begin circling with the second letter. Write out the answer on the blank lines provided.

YEMLREWCXTLR3OINX-MARTVT2REA#CLTCI8N+G
TPOOHWOERR9 I%S7 CTA+LRLWEND6
EOLAEUCITGREOHNPEOGQAUTUITVSIETGYR.
STOHPER   MROAR2E
CE4LME8C.T$RTO6NHE,GXA%TVI'VNE BAJNE
EKLCERMAEUNIT SIESE, JTLHPEI   M+OGR$E
HI1T5 WDADNOTUSE TMO XSNTNE3A'L=
ETLXENCRTERAOENWSD!B!

_____

_____

_____

When a molecule is made of two or more different kinds of atoms, we call the molecule a **compound**. We use chemical compounds every day—such as sugar, salt, and water. A compound's ingredients never change. For example, water always is made up of two hydrogen atoms and one oxygen atom, whether the water is found in the United States, in China, or on Mars.

Molecule Match Up, Part 1

As you know, molecules are made of the atoms. Below you'll find both descriptions and pictures of molecules. Match 'em up! On the next page are more molecules to match up.

This molecule is made of two atoms of hydrogen (H) and one atom of oxygen (O). •

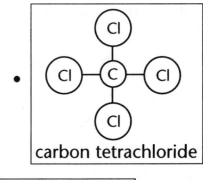

carbon tetrachloride

This molecule has two carbon (C) atoms and • six hydrogen atoms.

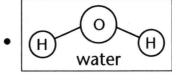

water

In this compound, you'll find only one carbon atom but • four chlorine atoms.

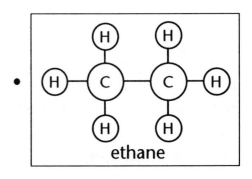

ethane

Do you remember reading about each of the words below? When you think you know the meaning of a word, put a ✓ in the box next to it.

- ❑ **chemical bond**
- ❑ **ionic bond**
- ❑ **covalent bond**
- ❑ **molecule**
- ❑ **ion**
- ❑ **compound**

Benzene is a compound made from petroleum. It's used in many products, including insecticides and detergents. Chloroform is another common substance. It has many uses, including keeping food cool in refrigerators.

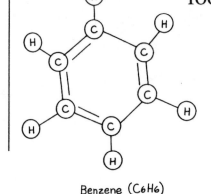

Benzene (C6H6)

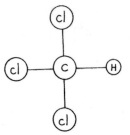

Chloroform (CHCl₃)

Molecule Match Up, Part 2

This simple compound has an atom of nitrogen (N) in it, plus three atoms of hydrogen.

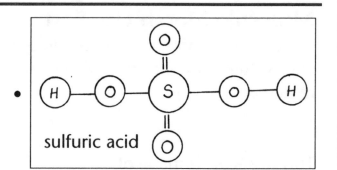

sulfuric acid

This molecule is more complicated: It has an atom of calcium (Ca), an atom of carbon, and three atoms of oxygen.

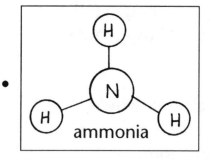

ammonia

Here's another complicated compound. It has two atoms of hydrogen, one of sulfur (S), and four of oxygen.

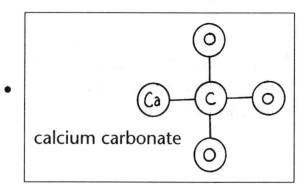

calcium carbonate

Not All Compounds Are Alike ◄·······

A salt molecule is different than a sugar molecule is different than a soap molecule, right? The big question is: *Why* do different molecules have different properties? That question has two answers:

❶ Different compounds are made of atoms of different elements, and as you've learned, different elements behave differently. Water, for instance, is very different than propane.

What's the Difference?

The difference between a molecule and a compound is this: A compound is a substance made up of two or more elements, while a molecule is a substance made up of two or more atoms. So, O_2 is a molecule but not a compound. Why? Because it has only one type of element (oxygen).

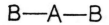

B—A—B

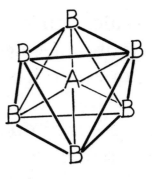

❷ Different compounds have different arrangements of their atoms. The way a molecule is put together—its molecular structure—makes all the difference in how it behaves.

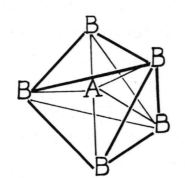

What Am I?

Can you solve the riddles below? Give it a try! (If you need help, go back and "CHECK OUT THE SCIENCE WORDS" on pages 9, 17, 23 and 27.)

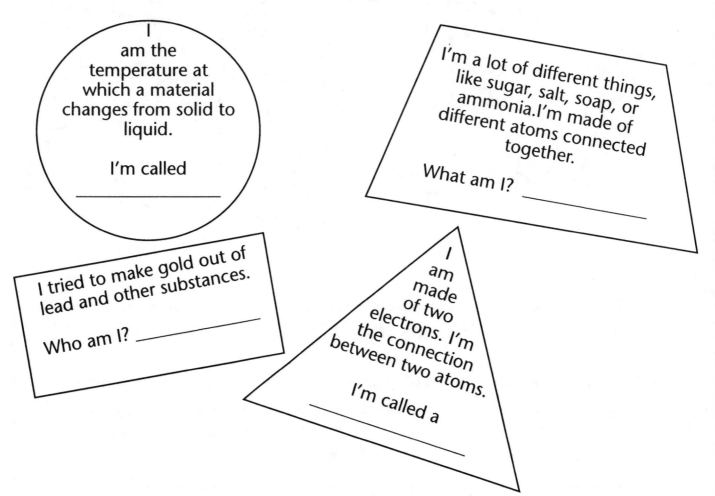

I am the temperature at which a material changes from solid to liquid.

I'm called

_____

I'm a lot of different things, like sugar, salt, soap, or ammonia. I'm made of different atoms connected together.

What am I? _____

I tried to make gold out of lead and other substances.

Who am I? _____

I am made of two electrons. I'm the connection between two atoms.

I'm called a

_____

When we talk more about chemical reactions later in this book, you'll see just how important molecular structure is. For now, let's concentrate on how structure is important to a compound's properties, or qualities.

Take a look at the structures of these two carbon compounds, both of which are crystals:

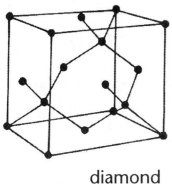

diamond

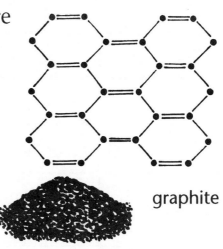

graphite

Puzzling Crossword

This crossword puzzle is a little different. There are no ACROSS and DOWN clues. Instead, you'll find letters in the puzzle, and these are your clues as to where the words go. Each word from the Word Box fits in the puzzle. Good luck!

Word Box

benzene
chemical
chloroform
compound
covalent
bond
ion
ionic bond
petroleum
structure

While both diamond and graphite contain only carbon atoms, their atoms aren't put together the same way. That changes everything. The two structures, diamond and graphite, end up having different properties, as the table shows below.

Properties	diamond	graphite
form	an extremely hard solid	a soft solid
color	colorless or white	steel gray to black
appearance	highly refractive	dull

How Many Atoms?

In this counting game, you need to figure out how many atoms there are in each molecule. Remember that when you see a number in a molecule, like the number 2 in H_2O, it means the molecule has that many atoms of that element. So, water has 2 atoms of hydrogen (H) and 1 atom of oxygen (O). Start counting! The first one is done for you.

1. NH_3 (ammonia) has __1__ nitrogen (N) atom(s) and __3__ hydrogen atom(s), for a total of __4__ atoms.

2. CO_2 (carbon dioxide) has ____ carbon (C) atom(s) and ____ oxygen atom(s), for a total of ____ atoms.

3. C_8H_{18} (octane) makes up our gasoline. Octane has ____ carbon atoms and ____ hydrogen atoms. In all, octane has ____ atoms.

There are three basic kinds of molecular structures:

❶ linear

In linear molecules, the atoms form a straight line, like this:

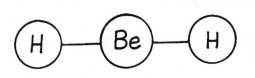

❷ trigonal planar

A trigonal planar molecule looks like a triangle, with an atom at the center. The atoms are arranged as if on a flat surface.

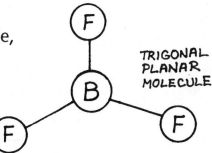

TRIGONAL PLANAR MOLECULE

4. $AgNO_3$ is the formula for silver nitrate. This chemical has ____ silver (Ag) atom(s), ____ nitrogen (N) atom(s), and ____ oxygen atoms.

5. Here's a tougher one. Methanol, a kind of alcohol, looks like this: CH_3OH. Methanol has ____ carbon atom(s), ____ hydrogen atom(s), and ____ oxygen atom(s).

6. Sulfuric acid (H_2SO_4) has a total of ____ atoms. Write out the names of each kind of element and how many atoms there are of each one:

element name	number of atoms
_____	_____
_____	_____
_____	_____

❸ tetrahedral

Look at the tetrahedral molecule. It has a center atom, with four atoms connected to it, stretching out in different directions.

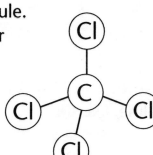

CHECK OUT THE
SCIENCE WORDS!

Do you remember reading about each of the words below? When you think you know the meaning of a word, put a ✓ in the box next to it.

- ❑ **molecular structure**
- ❑ **linear**
- ❑ **trigonal planar**
- ❑ **tetrahedral**
- ❑ **three-dimensional**

Tetrahedral molecules are **three-dimensional**, or 3D for short. That means they have three directions—up and down, across, and out.

In the experiment on the next two pages, you'll have a chance to make these three different moleular structures.

34

Making Molecules C

It's much easier to understand molecular structure when you make models of them. It's a lot of fun, too! The molecules you'll make are called beryllium hydride, boron trifluoride, and methane.

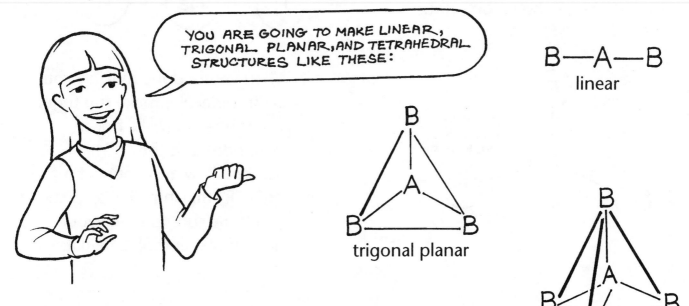

YOU ARE GOING TO MAKE LINEAR, TRIGONAL PLANAR, AND TETRAHEDRAL STRUCTURES LIKE THESE:

B—A—B
linear

trigonal planar

tetrahedral

What you'll need:
- 12 marshmallows
- 9 toothpicks
- colored markers

What to do:
1. Using a colored marker, write "Be" on one marshmallow, "H" on six marshmallows, "B" on one marshmallow, "F" on three marshmallows, and "C" on one marshmallow.

DO YOU HAVE ALL THE MARSHMALLOWS LABELLED?

THE "BE" STANDS FOR BERYLLIUM ELEMENT, "H" IS FOR HYDROGEN, "B" IS FOR BORON, "F" IS FOR FLUORINE AND "C" IS FOR CARBON.

2. Now make the beryllium hydride molecule. Take the one marshmallow labeled "Be" and two marshmallows labeled "H." Connect them with the toothpicks, as shown on right.

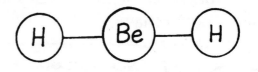

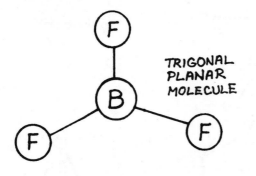

TRIGONAL PLANAR MOLECULE

3. When you're done making your linear molecule, make the trigonal planar one. To make boron trifluoride, take the "B" marshmallow and connect it to three "F" marshmallows, as shown on left. Be sure to make your trigonal planar molecule flat.

4. Now it's time for the hardest molecule: the tetrahedral. For this three-dimensional molecule, take the "C" marshmallow and the remaining four "H" marshmallows. Follow the picture carefully as you put your tetrahedral molecule together.

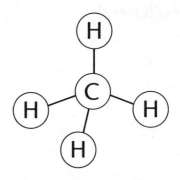

So how did you do? Good job. You're a chemist!

From This to That ◄ •

A LOT OF CHEMISTRY IS ABOUT **chemical change**. That's when a substance changes from one thing to another. Usually, one of two things happens:

❶ A substance breaks down into two or more substances.

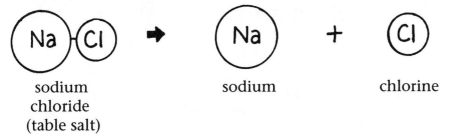

sodium
chloride
(table salt)   sodium   chlorine

❷ Two or more substances combine to form a new substance.

sodium   chlorine   sodium
                                    chloride
                                    (table salt)

Changes like these are called **chemical reactions**. In some reactions, substances break down *and* combine. Below, a strong acid and a strong base fall apart and combine again as two totally different and totally harmless substances.

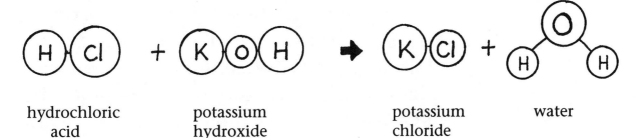

hydrochloric   potassium   potassium   water
acid   hydroxide   chloride

When chemists write down chemical reactions on paper, they're called **chemical equations**. The "equation" part means that everything on the left side of the arrow equals what's on the right side. If you take a good look at the chemical equation just below, you'll see that that's true: no atom is lost or gained.

Here's another look at that reaction:

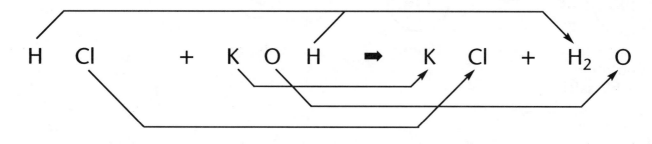

And here's a chemical reaction that's very important—if you happen to be in outer space, that is! Potassium superoxide reacts with carbon dioxide to make oxygen. That comes in handy inside space capsules, because astronauts need the oxygen to breathe.

$$4\,KO_2 \quad + \quad 2\,CO_2 \quad \Rightarrow \quad 2\,K_2CO_3 \quad + \quad 3\,O_2$$

potassium superoxide   carbon dioxide   potassium carbonate   oxygen

Do you notice how the molecules on the left side of the arrow break apart and then join togther as different molecules on the right side? Notice, too, how *four* molecules of KO_2 react with *two* molecules of CO_2 to make *two* molecules of K_2CO_3 and *three* molecules of O_2.

The next reaction is part of just about everyone's daily life. This particular reaction makes our cars go. In an automobile engine, gasoline reacts with oxygen molecules to produce carbon dioxide and water.

$$C_7H_{16} \quad + \quad 11\,O_2 \quad \Rightarrow \quad 7\,CO_2 \quad + \quad 8\,H_2O$$

gasoline   oxygen   carbon   water
                                            dioxide

The reaction of gasoline and oxygen is said to be **spontaneous**. That's because it will happen all on its own. (The reaction is very slow, but given enough time it will happen. In a car engine, the reaction is greatly speeded up.)

Draw Molecules

Are you ready to draw your own compounds? We'll start with something simple and linear, then work our way to more complex structures.

First, draw carbon dioxide. CO_2 is a linear molecule. It's also a gas found in our atmosphere. It's made of:

⇨   One carbon (C) atom at the center.
⇨   Two oxygen (O) atoms on either side
     of the carbon atom.   carbon dioxide

Next draw sulfur trioxide, a trigonal planar molecule. This molecule is a very poisonous smog gas that is damaging to our lungs.

⇨   One sulfur (S) atom at the center.
⇨   Three oxygen (O) atom around the S atom.   sulfur trioxide

Any reaction that will happen on its own is called spontaneous.

What about changing the reaction around so the substances on the left side of the equation are now on the right, like this?

$$7\,CO_2 \quad + \quad 8\,H_2O \quad \rightarrow \quad C_7H_{16} \quad + \quad 11\,O_2$$

Does this reaction happen? Will carbon dioxide and water react and form gasoline and oxygen? *Turn to page 43 to find out!*

Now it's time to draw a tetrahedral molecule. Carbon tetrachloride (CCl4) is a colorless, poisonous liquid that's used to dissolve other chemicals. Since it can't catch fire, it's also used in fire extinguishers. Draw carbon tetrachloride this way:

⇨ One carbon (C) atom at the center.

⇨ Three chlorine (Cl) atoms connected to the carbon atom. The chlorine atoms go out in different directions.

carbon tetrachloride

EXPERIMENT: Fizzy Fun C

As you've learned, a chemical reaction happens when molecules break apart to form new molecules. In this experiment, you'll see a chemical reaction that is pretty spectacular right before your very eyes!

What you'll need:
- baking soda
- vinegar
- a clear, clean drinking glass
- tablespoon
- teaspoon
- stirring spoon

What to do:
1. Start your experiment by putting one tablespoon of vinegar into the drinking glass.

STEP 1

STEP 2

2. Now comes the baking soda. Add one teaspoon of it to the glass.

3. Gently mix the vinegar and baking soda together by stirring them with a spoon. What happens? What do you see?

STEP 3

4. Write about your observations. _____

_____

_____

_____

_____

_____

_____

_____

_____

_____

What happened?

When you mixed the vinegar and baking soda, you started a chemical reaction. The equation for that reaction looks like this:

$$NaHCO_3 + HC_2H_3O_2 \rightarrow NaC_2H_3O_2 + H_2O + CO_2$$

baking   vinegar   sodium   water   carbon
soda   acetate   dioxide

The molecules on the left side of the arrow fell apart and recombined to make the molecules on the right side. Now, baking soda is a solid, and vinegar is a liquid. But these compounds disappeared when you mixed them. What appeared are sodium acetate (a solid), water (a liquid), and carbon dioxide (a gas). The sodium acetate, being a solid, was with the water. But what happened to the carbon dioxide? It did what gases do when they form inside a liquid. It tried to escape, because it's lighter than the liquid. So, it bubbled to the surface of the water. That's what all the foam in your experiment was—CO_2 escaping from the water!

Nope. The reaction of carbon dioxide and water to form gasoline and oxygen is *not* spontaneous. It will never happen, no matter how long we wait.

Sometimes, reactions are spontaneous both ways—that is, both the forward reaction and the reverse reaction will happen. For example, if you mix oxygen and hydrogen gases at room temperature (not heated up), most of the gas will remain together without reacting for years and years. But given enough time, the two gases *will* react and water *will* be made:

$$H_2 + H_2 + O_2 \rightarrow H_2O + H_2O$$

Right or Wrong?

Do you remember how in a chemical equation the substances on the left side of the arrow always equal what's on the right side? When they don't, you can bet the chemical equation is wrong. Checking whether a chemical equation is right is easy. Just make a quick chart. Take the reaction of baking soda and vinegar:

$$NaHCO_3 + HC_2H_3O_2 \rightarrow CO_2 + H_2O + NaC_2H_3O_2$$

Now make a chart:

How many:	are on the left?	are on the right?
Na	1	1
H	5	5
C	3	3
O	5	5

Now it's your turn. Go to the bottom of the next page.

The chart shows that the left and right sides of the equation have the same numbers of the same atoms. The equation is correct.

Do you remember reading about each of the words below? When you think you know the meaning of a word, put a ✓ in the box next to it.

❑ chemical change

❑ chemical reaction

❑ chemical equation

❑ spontaneous

The reverse reaction will happen, too:

$$H_2O + H_2O \rightarrow H_2 + H_2 + O_2$$

Over time, water will break down to form oxygen and hydrogen gas. Did you notice how in the chemical equation for the reverse reaction, the molecules switched sides?

> ### examples of chemical change
> • rust forming when the oxygen in the air reacts with iron, as in a nail, gate, or other object
> • wood changing into ashes after burning
> • a raw egg cooking into a hard-boiled egg
> • explosion of TNT (gun powder) and oxygen

Below are a bunch more chemical equations. Are they right or wrong? When one is right, but a ✔ beside it. When it's wrong, put an ✗ beside it. Use scratch paper to make your own charts.

✔ or ✗?

1. $C_3H_8 + O_2 \rightarrow CO_2 + H_2O$ ____

2. $Cu_2O + C \rightarrow Cu + CO_2$ ____

3. $Ag + S \rightarrow Ag_2S$ ____

4. $CH_3OH + O_2 \rightarrow HCOOH + H_2O$ ____

5. $CaCO_3 \rightarrow CaO + CO_2$ ____

6. $N_2 + H_2 + H_2 \rightarrow NH_3 + NH_3$ ____

7. $CH_3COOH + HOCH_2CH_3 \rightarrow CH_3COOCH_2CH_3 + H_2O$ ____

A Closer Look at Reactions ◄------

As you've learned, chemical reactions can take place really fast—in the blink of an eye—or they can take place really slowly, even over billions of years. So, a reaction can be spontaneous and fast or spontaneous and slow. Reactions that are spontaneous and *very* fast are called explosions.

But why is it that sometimes molecules don't react at all? Well, in chemical reactions, the way molecules approach each other is very important. That's because of their structure (remember that?). If the molecules don't "say hello" properly—if their positions

Structure Match Up

What do you remember about molecular structures? Match each kind of structure below with the correct picture on the right. (No peeking on earlier pages of this book!)

trigonal planar •

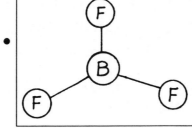

linear •

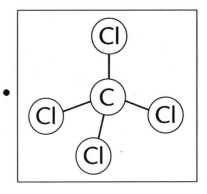

tetrahedral •

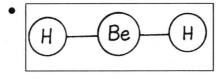

are off—then they won't be able to form something new.

You can think of it this way: The structures of the molecules have to hook up in just the right way so that their atoms can form a new bond with each other. We call that **orientation**—the way two things are positioned near each other.

Look at ethylene amine and water, especially the shaded carbon (C) and oxygen (O) atoms (these are the two atoms that want to react). If they are oriented the wrong way, they'll just bounce off each other.

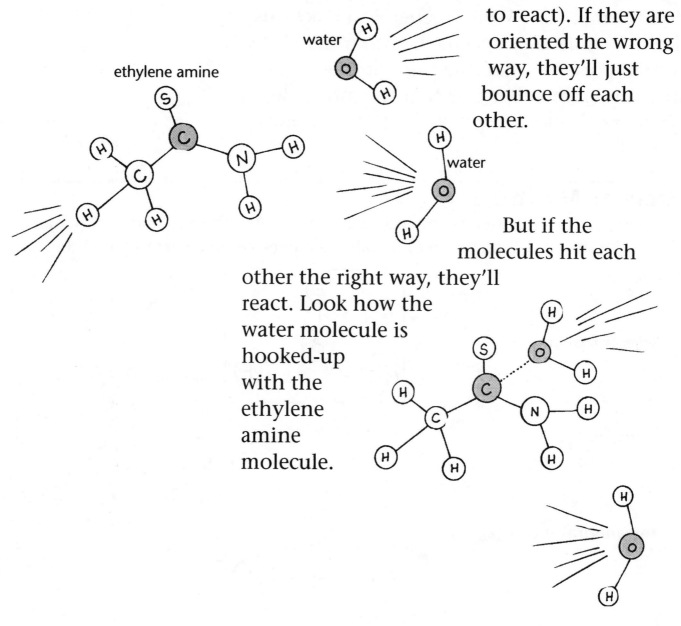

water

ethylene amine

water

But if the molecules hit each other the right way, they'll react. Look how the water molecule is hooked-up with the ethylene amine molecule.

The **energy level** of molecules is also important. When two molecules only lightly bump into each other because they have low energy, they may just bounce away and never react.

EXPERIMENT: Disappearing Sugar C

When you dissolve sugar into water, do you think it matters whether the water is warm or cold? Would it help out if the water were stirred? In this experiment, you're going to look at a single chemical reaction, but under four different conditions. Which reaction happens the fastest (in other words, which has the fastest rate of reaction)? Is temperature important? Is stirring? Let's find out.

What you'll need:
- four drinking glasses
- cold and warm water
- measuring cup
- timer (or clock with secondhand)
- sugar
- spoon

What to do:

1. Line up the four glasses side by side, as shown. So you won't get your glasses confused, put a label in front of each one. Copy the labels below.

1	2	3	4
cold	cold	warm	warm
stirred	not stirred	stirred	not stirred

CHECK OUT THE SCIENCE WORDS!

Do you remember reading about each of the words below? When you think you know the meaning of a word, put a ✓ in the box next to it.

❑ **orientation**

❑ **energy level**

But if the two molecules have a lot of energy, then they'll collide with a lot of force. When that happens, the molecules have a good chance of knocking atoms off each other and reacting. New molecules will form.

EXPERIMENT: Disappearing Sugar (continued)

2. Pour exactly one cup of water into each glass. To glasses 1 and 2, add cold water. To glasses 3 and 4, add warm water (from the tap is fine; do not use boiling water!).

3. For this next step, have your watch or timer handy. To each glass, add one leveled tablespoon of sugar. As soon as you're through, start measuring the time.

4. Quickly stir glasses 2 and 4 for 10 seconds. Watch all four glasses carefully. In which glass does the most sugar dissolve? In which the least? Which is more important, temperature or stirring, in dissolving the sugar?

5. Now describe what happened in your experiment and why. _____

_____

_____

_____

_____

48

Speed it Up! ←-------------------------------

WHEN A CHEMICAL REACTION is spontaneous but slow, a lot of times it's possible to speed up the process. Let's look at a few different ways reactions can be helped along.

❶ You can increase the concentration of the substances that are reacting. Concentration means how much stuff is crammed into a given amount of space.

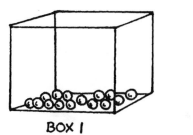
BOX 1

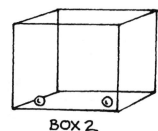
BOX 2

Which box has the higher concentration of marbles, box 1 or box 2? If you guessed box 1, you'd be right.

With a higher concentration, more molecules are colliding and reacting. So, with greater amounts of substances added together, the faster the reaction will be to form new substances.

CHECK OUT THE SCIENCE WORDS!

Do you remember reading about each of the words below? When you think you know the meaning of a word, put a ✓ in the box next to it.

❑ **concentration**

❑ **catalyst**

❷ You can raise the temperature of the substances reacting. When you do that, the molecules you are trying to get to react move *faster* because of the heat energy. Since they're moving faster, the molecules collide more often with each other, and the reaction goes faster.

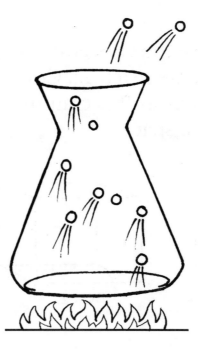

❸ Finally, you can speed up a reaction by adding a **catalyst** to it. A catalyst is a substance that helps a reaction go along faster by bringing the reacting substances together.

Living Chemistry

You and I, your friends and family, bugs and bats, flowers and trees, and any plant, animal, or other living thing you can think of are all living chemistry laboratories. That's because so many of chemical reactions happen inside all of us every minute of every day. These chemical reactions generate energy. They also make all kinds of new material needed for living things to grow and survive.

What's amazing is that all living things are made up of the same four compounds: **carbohydrates**, **lipids** (also called fats),

Riddle Time

Are you ready for some difficult riddles? Think hard and you'll be able to answer all of them!

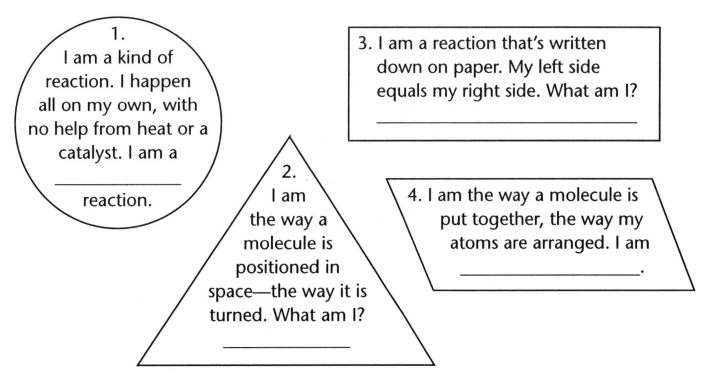

1.
I am a kind of reaction. I happen all on my own, with no help from heat or a catalyst. I am a

_____
reaction.

2.
I am the way a molecule is positioned in space—the way it is turned. What am I?

_____

3. I am a reaction that's written down on paper. My left side equals my right side. What am I?

_____

4. I am the way a molecule is put together, the way my atoms are arranged. I am

_____.

proteins, and **nucleic acids**. Lipids and carbohydrates are important energy-storage compounds. Proteins and nucleic acids play vital roles in growth and good health.

These four compounds, which have thousands of different jobs, are mainly made up of different combinations of just four elements: carbon, hydrogen, oxygen, and nitrogen.

Most living things also contain small amounts of these other elements: sulfur, phosphorous, chlorine, sodium, potassium, calcium, magnesium, and iron. All in all, there are about twenty elements found in living things. Of these, carbon is the coolest by far, because it is the only element that has

A Little H, A Little O

Circle every third letter (or symbol) in the puzzle below. Begin circling with the first letter. Write out the answer on the blank lines provided.

```
      WUIE  OEANAR89E3   &A9+LSELMU
W1JA0-LDAKB3ILDN8ZG6  3B2DAC-GVUSFN   OCBFE
            TA$U  VQPEADRIAY9
      3I6DMBAP(,OCDRPATUDAYHNEBTS@
        CSKOD4MUKPABOFSU1YNV8D2H:
        DHW4SAKOT19E&JRDD.   B$OKDU7LRA
  9BKLODXDXJIABECDSDI  AEIRPAEI   FMGDABCDB4E3
  1O*#FDK  MJKOFDR91E  KDTH+HHDAAUNI  B7C=0D$%
    3DHNA2UI0DX.E  NAC4MIVABBZA,IQ1N0DG3B!
```

_____

_____

_____

the chemical properties needed to make so many different, complex, and stable molecules. As a matter of fact, carbon is so important that we are all called "carbon life-forms."

In living things, two kinds of reactions are really important: **condensation** and **hydrolysis.** Condensation reactions build larger molecules from smaller ones. For example, starch, cellulose, and glycogen are all very large molecules made from smaller glucose molecules. Starch is the large sugar

Decode the Chemistry

To decode the message below, use the shape code presented on page 14. You'll learn something very interesting about what a catalyst can do.

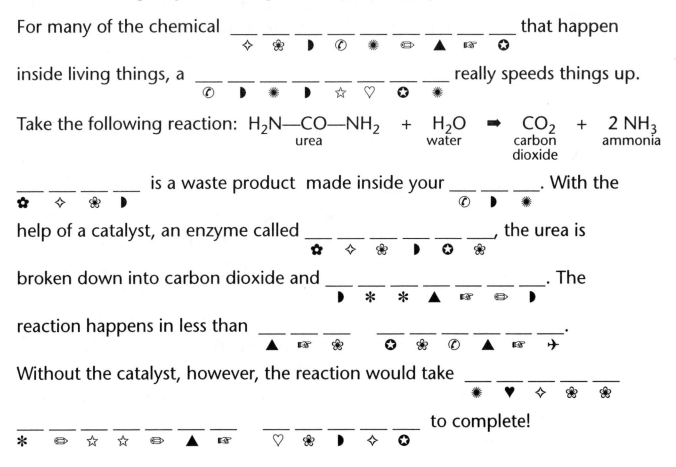

CHECK OUT THE SCIENCE WORDS!

Do you remember reading about each of the words below? When you think you know the meaning of a word, put a ✓ in the box next to it.

- ❑ **carbohydrates**
- ❑ **lipids**
- ❑ **proteins**
- ❑ **nucleic acids**
- ❑ **condensation**
- ❑ **hydrolysis**
- ❑ **enzyme**

molecule stored in plants. Cellulose molecules are what give plants their structural support. The woody parts of trees are made of cellulose, as are the stiff parts of grass and flowers. In animals, glycogen is a large energy molecule stored in the liver or in muscle tissue.

Hydrolysis reactions do the opposite of condensation reactions: They break down large molecules into smaller ones. Digestion is an example of hydrolysis. When you eat food, it is digested, or broken down, into smaller and smaller molecules until they're small enough for your body to absorb.

In our bodies, many reactions happen with the help of special protein molecules called **enzymes**. An enzyme acts as a catalyst, which means it helps to speed up a chemical reaction. For example, the food we eat are broken down by digestive enzymes. Without these enzymes, it woud take about 50 years to digest just one meal!

In this book, you have learned a lot about chemistry—including atoms and elements, molecules and compounds, molecular structures and chemical reactions. Are you ready to test what you know? When you turn the page, you'll see some definitions. Each one goes with a word from the Word Box. If you do a good job matching them up, a certificate is waiting for you at the end of the book!

Mix-Up Match-Up

Each of the words in the Word Box has a definition it belongs with. You'll find these definitions below. Match up the words and definitions by filling in the blanks.

1. _____: A molecule that has a center atom, with four atoms attached to it, reaching out in different directions.

2. _____: A quality, or characteristic, of an object, such as hardness, color, or weight.

Word Box

proton
tanning
chemical
tetrahedral
ion
nucleus
property
density
catalyst
reaction
element
condensation
trigonal
planar

3. _____: A substance, a material.

4. _____: A chemical change that involves a substance breaking down into other substances, or two substances combining to form a new substance.

5. _____: A chemical reaction that builds large molecules from smaller ones.

6. _____: The process of making leather out of animal skins.

7. _____: The positively charged particle inside an atom's nucleus.

8. _____: A substance that speeds up a reaction by bringing the reacting substances close together.

9. _____: A pure substance.

10. _____: A flat molecule that has a center atom, with three atoms attached to it.

11. _____: An atom or molecule with a positive or negative charge.

12. _____: This property of substances has to do with how tightly packed a substance's atoms are.

13. _____: The center of an atom, containing protons and neutrons.

Answer Sheet

Page 6
Answers will vary.

Page 7
1. c   3. a   5. b
2. d   4. e

Page 9
There are many possible answers. One is as follows:

	LEAD	
step 1	LEND	(A changed to N)
step 2	LAND	(E changed to A)
step 3	HAND	(L changed to H)
step 4	HARD	(N changed to R)
step 5	CARD	(H changed to C)
step 6	CORD	(A changed to O)
step 7	COLD	(R changed to L)
step 8	GOLD	(C changed to G)

Page 10
WATER DO NOT BURN. TREE BURN TOO FAST.

Page 11
1. Chemistry is a science.
2. Chemistry is about why and how substances are different from each other.
3. It is not possible to change one element into another element.
4. Lead was one of the substances that alchemists tried to turn into gold.

Page 14
ALUMINUM   SODIUM
MANGANESE   CESIUM
CALIFORNIUM   LITHIUM
TITANIUM   RUBIDIUM

Page 17
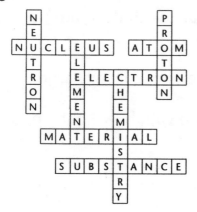

Page 18
The lightest cube is sugar, and the heaviest is iron. From lowest to highest density, the cubes should be ordered as follows: sugar, ice, silver, and iron.

Page 21

```
A C T I O R K W Z P A S O
L U X S H A P E O R B O S
T G D I M Z E I R O S M I
U M E L T I N G T E M P U
R K N S H U O H O T E T H
L W S U M C V T R I L K A
T E I S I D I H C O L O R
E E T H M V M O T E I A D
A M Y O C T E T E R Y Z N
D O U R B R E T S O M M E
I R R T S H I N I N E S S
S C O M R C O R Z E I K S
B O I L I N G T E M P E R
```

Page 22
From softest ⇨ hardest.
④ sandpaper ① fur   ③ soil   ② leaf

From lightest ⇨ heaviest.
① flour   ② sugar   ③ cooking oil   ④ honey

From dullest ⇨ shiniest.
③ marble   ① wood   ② concrete   ④ glass

From least transparent ⇨ most transparent.
② paper   ① aluminum foil ④ glass   ③ plastic

Page 24
Remember this **warning**. When you grow up and are working in a **laboratory**, don't place **sodium**, not even a little tiny piece of it, in **water**. If you do, you might have an **explosion**. That's because this metal has just a single outer **electron**, which the **oxygen** in a **water** molecule loves to **steal**. In fact, the **oxygen** steals the **electron** quite violently. The **sodium** and **water** molecules react to form **sodium** hydroxide and **hyrogen** gas. The reaction also creates a lot of heat, so much so that the **hydrogen** gas may catch **fire**— KABOOM!

Page 26
Electron-attracting power is called electronegativity. The more electronegative an element is, the more it wants to steal electrons!

Answer Sheet

Page 27-28

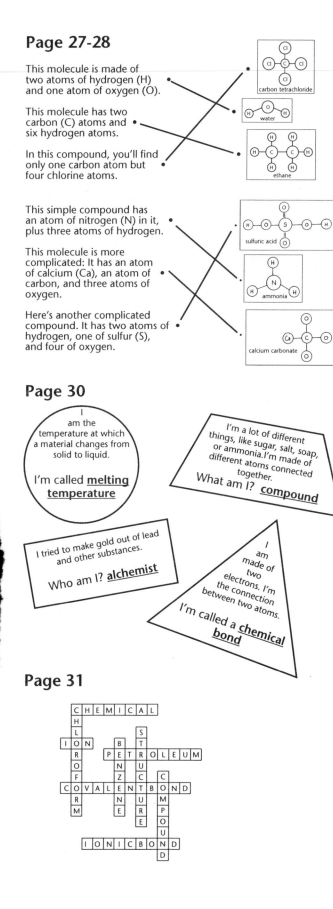

This molecule is made of two atoms of hydrogen (H) and one atom of oxygen (O).

This molecule has two carbon (C) atoms and six hydrogen atoms.

In this compound, you'll find only one carbon atom but four chlorine atoms.

This simple compound has an atom of nitrogen (N) in it, plus three atoms of hydrogen.

This molecule is more complicated: It has an atom of calcium (Ca), an atom of carbon, and three atoms of oxygen.

Here's another complicated compound. It has two atoms of hydrogen, one of sulfur (S), and four of oxygen.

carbon tetrachloride

water

ethane

sulfuric acid

ammonia

calcium carbonate

Page 30

I am the temperature at which a material changes from solid to liquid.

I'm called **melting temperature**

I'm a lot of different things, like sugar, salt, soap, or ammonia. I'm made of different atoms connected together.
What am I? **compound**

I tried to make gold out of lead and other substances.

Who am I? **alchemist**

I am made of two electrons. I'm the connection between two atoms.
I'm called a **chemical bond**

Page 31

```
C H E M I C A L
H
L           S
I O N     B   T
R     P E T R O L E U M
O       N   U
F       Z   C   C
C O V A L E N T B O N D
R       N   U   M
M       E   R   P
            E   O
                U
    I O N I C B O N D
                D
```

Page 32-33

1. NH_3 (ammonia) has __1__ nitrogen (N) atom(s) and __3__ hydrogen atom(s), for a total of __4__ atoms.

2. CO_2 (carbon dioxide) has __1__ carbon (C) atom(s) and __2__ oxygen atom(s), for a total of __3__ atoms.

3. C_8H1_8 (octane) makes up our gasoline. Octane has __8__ carbon atoms and __18__ hydrogen atoms. In all, octane has __26__ atoms.

4. $AgNO_3$ is the formula for silver nitrate. This chemical has __1__ silver (Ag) atoms, __1__ nitrogen (N) atom(s), and __3__ oxygen atoms.

5. Here's a tougher one. Methanol, a kind of alcohol, looks like this: CH_3OH. Methanol has __1__ carbon atom(s), __4__ hydrogen atom(s), and __1__ oxygen atom(s).

6. Sulfuric acid (H_2SO_4) has a total of __7__ atoms. Write out the names of each kind of element and how many atoms there are of each one:

element name	number of atoms
hydrogen	2
sulfur	1
oxygen	4

Page 39

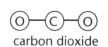

carbon dioxide

sulfur trioxide

Page 40

carbon tetrachloride

Page 44

1. ✗	3. ✗	5. ✓	7. ✓
2. ✗	4. ✓	6. ✗	

Answer Sheet

Page 45

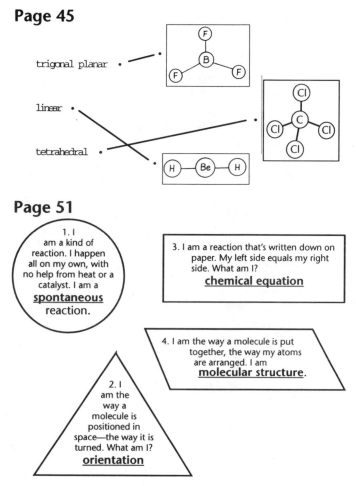

trigonal planar

linear

tetrahedral

Page 51

1. I am a kind of reaction. I happen all on my own, with no help from heat or a catalyst. I am a **spontaneous** reaction.

3. I am a reaction that's written down on paper. My left side equals my right side. What am I? **chemical equation**

4. I am the way a molecule is put together, the way my atoms are arranged. I am **molecular structure**.

2. I am the way a molecule is positioned in space—the way it is turned. What am I? **orientation**

Page 52

We are all walking bags of a very important compound: water. Our bodies are made of more than 70% water. Amazing!

Page 53

For many of the chemical r e a c t i o n s that happen inside living things, a c a t a l y s t really speeds things up.

Take the following reaction:

$$H_2N–CO–NH_2 + H_2O \rightarrow CO_2 + 2\,NH_3$$

urea   water   carbon dioxide   ammonia

u r e a is a waste product made inside your c a t . With the help of a catalyst, an enzyme called u r e a s e , the urea is broken down into carbon dioxide and a m m o n i a . The reaction happens in less than o n e   s e c o n d . Without the catalyst, however, the reaction would take t h r e e   m i l l i o n   y e a r s to complete!

Page 55

1. tetrahedral
2. property
3. chemical
4. reaction
5. condensation
6. tanning
7. proton
8. catalyst
9. element
10. trigonal planar
11. ion
12. density
13. nucleus